The Global Economy
America and the World

**HUGH ROOME AND
ANNE ROSS ROOME**

Children's Press®
An Imprint of Scholastic Inc.
New York Toronto London Auckland Sydney
Mexico City New Delhi Hong Kong
Danbury, Connecticut

Content Consultant
Rodney Shrader, PhD
Professor, Denton Thorne Chair in Entrepreneurship
University of Illinois–Chicago
Chicago, Illinois

Library of Congress Cataloging-in-Publication Data
Roome, Hugh.
 The global economy : America and the world / Hugh Roome and Anne Ross Roome.
 pages cm.—(A true book)
 Includes bibliographical references and index.
 ISBN 978-0-531-24776-1 (lib. bdg.) — ISBN 978-0-531-28462-9 (pbk.)
 1. International trade—Juvenile literature. 2. International economic relations—Juvenile literature.
 3. Globalization—Economic aspects—Juvenile literature. 4. United States—Commerce—Juvenile
 literature. I. Roome, Anne Ross. II. Title.
 HF1379.R66 2014
 337—dc23   2013014252

All rights reserved. Published in 2014 by Children's Press, an imprint of Scholastic Inc.
Printed in China 62
SCHOLASTIC, CHILDREN'S PRESS, A TRUE BOOK™, and associated logos are trademarks and/or
registered trademarks of Scholastic Inc.
1 2 3 4 5 6 7 8 9 10 R 23 22 21 20 19 18 17 16 15 14

Front cover: Woman holding a globe
Back cover: Puzzle globe

Find the Truth!

Everything you are about to read is true *except* for one of the sentences on this page.

Which one is **TRUE**?

T or F The United States produces more movies than any other country.

T or F Globalism took place thousands of years ago.

Find the answers in this book.

Contents

THE **BIG** TRUTH!

Outsourcing

ON'T

TSOURCE

McDonald's has restaurants in more than 100 different countries.

By 2013, there were nearly 400 Apple Stores worldwide.

CHAPTER 1

Shrinking the Globe

The world is getting smaller! These days, people, goods, and ideas can easily travel from one side of the world to the other. This is part of a trend called **globalization**. It allows people around the world to connect, whether to share ideas or to buy or sell goods and services. Modern technology, such as airplanes and the Internet, has made global trade and communication fast and easy.

More than 1 billion smartphones were sold around the world between 2007 and 2012.

One Big Neighborhood

A boy in Egypt kicks a soccer ball around with a group of friends. A girl in Alaska dances to the music of Shakira playing on her computer. A woman in Argentina drives to work in a car made in Japan. A man in Germany sits down with a bowl of popcorn to watch a movie in French.

These people live thousands of miles apart. What do they have in common?

Many people in Mozambique and around the world start playing soccer at an early age.

Some french fries are made in one country and cooked and eaten in another.

People around the world share sports, movies, music, technology, and even food. T-shirts and sneakers are made in one part of the world and worn by people in another. Pieces of cars and computers are made in one place, assembled in another, and sold across the globe. These products are so widely available because of globalization. However, globalization is far from new.

Alexander the Great invaded India in 327 BCE.

Ancient Roots

Thousands of years ago, people began leaving their villages and farms to explore other places. In the fourth century BCE, Alexander the Great took over lands surrounding Greece to create an empire. Alexander and his military introduced Greek trade, art, and government to the conquered nations. At the same time, the Greeks picked up local styles and practices. This is one of the earliest known examples of globalization.

The Roman Empire connected parts of the world through conquest about 2,000 years ago. The Romans and the people they conquered traded knowledge of math and science, road-building and shipbuilding methods, and other technologies. Many people learned to speak Latin, the language of the Romans. As a result, people from a wide range of lands could have conversations and share ideas. (It was not all good. The Romans also stole property and turned thousands of people into slaves.)

Latin developed into modern Italian, French, Spanish, Portuguese, and Romanian.

This map shows the reach of the Roman Empire at its height.

The Silk Road

For more than a thousand years, cloth, spices, and other goods were carried between Europe and Asia along the Silk Road. This international trade route was 4,000 miles (6,400 kilometers) long. Popular goods that only came from certain places fetched the highest prices. For example, Europeans loved black

pepper, but it was grown in Asia. It took months to transport it to Europe. As a result, pepper was almost as expensive as gold in Europe.

The Silk Road stopped being used around the 14th century.

The Growth of Global Transportation

Early traders moved goods using camels, horses, wagons, small ships, and people. It took months to travel between China and Europe. Goods were often transferred from one trader to the next along the way. It was rare that one person made the entire journey. Roads, ground transport, and ships gradually improved over the centuries. From the 15th century onward, ships sailed between Europe, Asia, Africa, and the Americas, carrying people, raw materials, and finished products.

CHAPTER 2

Business Goes Global

Technology has come a long way since ancient times. Today, jets move people and products farther in three hours than an ancient Roman could travel in a month. One modern ship can travel 10 times faster than a Roman ship and carry more than 1,000 times the load. Highways and railways make crossing continents fast and inexpensive. Communication across almost any distance is easy, thanks to telephones and the Internet.

← It takes just 23 hours to fly from New York City to Singapore.

Becoming International

With the help of these advancements in technology, global businesses have flourished. Transporting raw materials and finished products in and out of countries is fast and affordable. Company offices and factories around the world can communicate with buyers, sellers, and each other. This results in easier access to materials, workers, and **markets** globally.

Phones help company officials stay up to date on factory production.

Apple Inc.'s apple logo was first designed in 1977.

Brands

Companies that are recognizable and memorable to consumers often sell more products. To achieve this, companies come up with a **brand** name. Brands are made more identifiable with a simple **logo**. Apple Inc.'s unique apple artwork and the Walt Disney Company's castle are two examples. Companies build their brand so that their name and logo are recognizable anywhere, no matter what a consumer's language is.

By 2013, McDonald's had more than 34,000 restaurants around the world.

Global Food

When they first opened in the mid-1900s, American food **chains** such as McDonald's had restaurants only in the United States. Now you can eat food from McDonald's, Wendy's, and other restaurants in dozens of countries around the world. This isn't limited to American restaurants. For example, you can visit the United Kingdom's Pret A Manger restaurants in the United States, France, and Hong Kong.

Playtime

LEGO interlocking bricks were created in the 1950s by the LEGO Company in Denmark. Around the same time, the company began **exporting** to Sweden and other nearby nations. Today, LEGO bricks are available everywhere and are one of the world's most popular toys.

As LEGOs were getting started, Disneyland was being built in California. Since then, Disney parks have expanded not only to Florida but also to China, Hong Kong, and France.

Many people around the world have made LEGO models of cities, landmarks, people, and objects.

Different People, Different Things

Companies sometimes need to change their products to sell them in other countries. McDonald's does not sell hamburgers in India because many Indians don't eat beef. Instead, McDonald's offers sandwiches made with chicken, fish, vegetables, or even *paneer*, a kind of cheese. Company employees traveling to other countries face differences in language. Differences in culture can be another obstacle. For instance, it is considered impolite in Korea for a person to shake hands with one hand in his or her pocket.

Bill Gates made international news in 2013 when he shook hands with South Korea's President Park Geun-hye while keeping his left hand in his pocket.

20

The Boeing factory in Everett, Washington, is the largest building on Earth.

Airplanes built by Boeing and other manufacturers include parts made around the world.

Gathering Materials

To build products, companies need a workforce and materials. A business might find it easiest and cheapest to use resources that are at hand. Individual parts and assembled products may all be made in the same country. However, today's transportation and communication technologies make resources in other places very accessible. As a result, many products are made with parts built by suppliers around the world.

21

Apple Inc. uses parts built by suppliers based in Asia, Europe, and the United States to assemble the iPhone. This practice can be good for the business because each part comes from a country that is best at making that part. Car manufacturers such as Japan's Toyota Motor Corporation not only use international parts but also own factories around the globe. Toyota manufactures cars in nearly 30 different countries in Europe, Asia, Africa, the Americas, and Australia.

Timeline of Globalization

336 BCE
Alexander the Great begins to spread his empire.

Around 300 BCE
Traders begin traveling along the Silk Road.

27 BCE
Julius Caesar establishes the Roman Empire.

The big jets that fly around the world are also made in many countries. An Airbus 380-800 airplane has parts from Britain, Germany, France, and elsewhere. Boeing's new Dreamliner is also a global plane. Its wings are made in Japan, its doors in France and Sweden, and its engines in Britain. Some of these airplane parts are huge. Special ships and transport planes bring the pieces to a factory where they can be assembled.

1967 CE
McDonald's opens its first restaurant outside the United States.

1983
The first Disneyland outside the United States, Disneyland Tokyo, opens.

Outsourcing

Parts are not the only thing that can be international. Jobs can also move. Perhaps workers in Africa are willing to work for a U.S. company for less money than American workers in the United States. If the job can be done through computer or by telephone, then the company may choose to hire workers in Africa. This is called outsourcing.

Outsourcing has led to disagreements among people, companies, and even countries. While creating jobs in one country, it reduces the number of jobs available in another. With fewer jobs available, more people struggle to make ends meet. However, outsourcing can make a company's products more affordable for consumers. Companies and governments have to weigh the potential gains and losses when deciding whether to outsource.

CHAPTER 3

Global Entertainment

Entertainment comes in many forms—movies, music, books, sports, and more. They are sometimes called global properties because people all over the world can enjoy them. Movies such as the Star Wars and Harry Potter films are watched by hundreds of millions of people. Books, movies, music, and other forms of **intellectual property** can be sold around the world, just like cars and food.

← The Harry Potter books have been translated into 74 languages.

Global Movies

When you think of movies, you may think of Hollywood, a very American business. However, movies are made everywhere. In fact, more movies are made in India than in the United States. Foreign films are often shown at theaters around the world and are sometimes highlighted at special film festivals. Subtitles can be added to movies so that anyone can watch, even if he or she doesn't speak the language used.

The Indian film industry is nicknamed Bollywood.

Digital music sales are constantly growing as they become available in more countries around the world.

Global Music

Until about 100 years ago, you could only hear music that was played live in front of you. Today, artists such as England's Adele, South Korea's Psy, France's David Guetta, and Canada's Justin Bieber are heard around the world. Artists can sell songs or show videos online, making it easier than ever before for consumers to access their music. Songs can be as popular in Korea, Mexico, or the United States as they are in their home country.

David Beckham takes a penalty kick in a World Cup match against Argentina in 2002.

Global Sports

The fact that we can watch sports around the world means that athletes and teams have fans everywhere. The most popular sport in the world is soccer. Originating in England in the 1800s, soccer has since spread around the world. Today, some of the best players come from Europe, Africa, South America, and Asia. Some even become celebrities. British player David Beckham is a superstar who has played for teams in the United Kingdom, Spain, and the United States.

The Olympic Games are a global event. The Olympics started in ancient Greece in 776 BCE, nearly 3,000 years ago. The modern Olympics are a peaceful, global athletic competition that brings countries together. Athletes from more than 200 countries compete every two years. More than 4 billion people watch the games on TV. Because of this, someone such as Michael Phelps from the United States—winner of 18 Olympic gold medals for swimming—is famous everywhere on Earth.

Michael Phelps has won a record 22 Olympic medals.

Traveling the Globe

Globalization has made it easier and cheaper to see the world. When we visit new places, whether another city or another country, we are tourists. One of the biggest businesses in the world is global tourism. One billion tourists spend a total of $1 trillion on travel each year. This creates jobs for local people in hotels, restaurants, and museums. It also gives visitors and locals an opportunity to better understand people from different countries.

Tourists support a range of businesses and their employees, such as restaurants and restaurant workers.

International Support

France is the world's most visited country. Nearly 80 million people visit there each year. For countries such as France, tourism is a big part of the economy. People travel to France to see great churches and castles built hundreds of years ago. They spend money to take tours of these places, which supports the upkeep of the sites. Tourists also pay to eat at restaurants and to stay at hotels. Rental cars, taxis, and public transportation get a boost from tourists, as well.

CHAPTER 4

Global Conflicts

Airplanes and tourism are not the only products of globalization. War can take on a global scale. The deadliest and widest-reaching example is World War II (1939–1945). One hundred million soldiers from every inhabited continent fought. The armies of the world used many businesses and technologies to fight. The most powerful weapon ever used—the atomic bomb—was exploded.

Five countries took part in the D-Day invasion of Normandy, France, in June 1944.

The United Nations

After World War II, about 50 countries got together to form the United Nations (UN) to help prevent future global wars. Today, representatives from 193 countries meet in New York City and elsewhere to work for world peace. The UN also provides food and medicine to people in need. The organization has its own international military, whose members are called peacekeepers. The UN does not solve all arguments, but it has helped prevent another world war.

The UN General Assembly meets at least once a year at the United Nations Headquarters in New York City.

Dutch military forces talk with local authorities in Uruzgan Province in Afghanistan.

The Global War on Terror

Though wars on the scale of World War II have been avoided, not all conflict has ended. Terrorism is a form of global conflict. For example, a terrorist group based in Asia attacked sites in the United States on September 11, 2001. The attack inspired an international effort, led by the United States, to stop that group and similar ones. The forces of several nations including the United Kingdom, France, and the Netherlands, have taken part.

CHAPTER 5

The Good and the Bad of Globalization

As business goes global, so does pollution. Ships, planes, and trucks carrying products around the world pollute the air, water, and land as they burn fuel for power. Economic growth, especially in places such as China and India, means more factories and a population that can afford to buy more things, including cars. Cars and factories produce smoke and chemicals, releasing the **toxins** into the air and water.

Air pollution includes both visible and invisible toxins.

An Expensive Problem

Pollution costs money. It causes health issues such as asthma and cancer, which means more people need medical treatment. Employees miss work, which costs businesses money. In China alone, a study found that pollution causes $75 billion each year in health costs. As a result, governments and businesses are looking for ways to "go green." International organizations such as the World Bank and the UN support their efforts with funding, research, and technology.

The International Water Association works to educate people and improve water management practices around the world.

40

UNICEF was founded in 1946 to help people facing disease and hunger after World War II.

Global Good

People are also finding new opportunities in globalization. When people around the world share ideas, things can improve. Scientists around the world are working together to advance medical knowledge. As a result, people almost everywhere are living longer. Deadly illnesses such as malaria, which kills 1.2 million people a year, can be cured with medicines that are now shared among countries. Improvements in water treatment and farming techniques have resulted in fewer people facing **malnutrition**.

Many adults go back to school at night or on weekends to learn new skills.

A Chance to Learn

As global businesses grow and develop, the need for education grows. Knowing different languages is important for people to communicate internationally. Basic workplace knowledge, such as how to use a computer, is also essential. Outsourcing makes finding a job even more competitive, so a good education is important. Paid online learning has been available for many years. But education has started expanding to include free online courses.

Free lessons can be as simple as a YouTube video teaching a guitar chord or as advanced as a physics lecture from Stanford University. Companies such as Advanced Learning Interactive Systems Online (ALISON) publish free courses on anything from workplace safety to psychology. Programs like these make quality education freely available.

While we battle problems caused by globalization, we also continue to find new opportunities in it. Globalization continues to change. What will it bring tomorrow? ★

Online lectures and lessons can be accessed by anyone with an Internet connection.

True Statistics

Number of people who travel to other countries each year: 1 billion

Number of passengers on an Airbus 380-800 airplane: Up to 853

Approximate length of the Silk Road, between Asia and Europe: 4,000 miles (6,400 km)

Number of countries competing in the Olympic Games: More than 200

Number of people who watch the Olympic Games: 4 billion, or 70 percent of all people

Number of people who fought in World War II: About 100 million soldiers

Did you find the truth?

F The United States produces more movies than any other country.

T Globalism took place thousands of years ago.

Resources

Books

Mara, Wil. *American Entrepreneurship*. New York: Children's Press, 2014.

Pavlovic, Zoran. *The Changing Global Economy*. New York: Chelsea House Publishers, 2009.

Yomtov, Nel. *Starting Your Own Business*. New York: Children's Press, 2014.

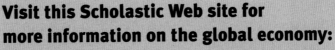

Visit this Scholastic Web site for more information on the global economy:
★ www.factsfornow.scholastic.com
Enter the keywords **Global Economy**

Important Words

brand (BRAND) — a name that identifies a product or the company that makes it

chains (CHAYNZ) — groups of stores or restaurants that are owned by the same company and sell similar products

exporting (EK-sport-ing) — sending products to another country to sell them there

globalization (gloh-buhl-uh-ZAY-shuhn) — the development of an economy in which nations around the world interact

intellectual property (in-tuh-LEK-choo-uhl PRAH-pur-tee) — an idea, invention, creative work, or process that derives from the work of the mind

logo (LOH-goh) — a distinctive symbol that identifies a particular company or organization

malnutrition (mal-noo-TRISH-uhn) — sickness or weakness caused by not eating enough food

markets (MAHR-kits) — groups of potential customers for a product or service

outsourcing (OUT-sors-ing) — moving a job to a place where hiring workers is cheaper

toxins (TAHK-sinz) — things that are poisonous

Index

Page numbers in **bold** indicate illustrations

About the Authors

Hugh Roome has a doctorate in international studies. He is an adjunct professor teaching a course on global risks and opportunities at New York University's School of Continuing and Professional Studies. He is currently an executive at Scholastic Inc.

Anne Ross Roome is a student of globalization. She has studied the way globalization can create opportunities for poor people but also increase problems such as pollution. She lives in the rural town of Greenwich, New York.